Contents

Introduction

APP level grids   5

Task 1	**Ready, Steady Scoff!**	Teacher sheet	8
		Pupil sheet	9
		Assessment grid	10
Task 2	**Seed Triathlon**	Teacher sheet	11
		Pupil sheet	12
		Assessment grid	13
Task 3	**A Lighter Loaf**	Teacher sheet	14
		Pupil sheet	15
		Assessment grid	16
Task 4	**Soggy Socks**	Teacher sheet	17
		Pupil sheet	18
		Assessment grid	19
Task 5	**Out of this World!**	Teacher sheet	20
		Pupil sheet	21
		Assessment grid	22
Task 6	**Good Vibrations**	Teacher sheet	23
		Pupil sheet	24
		Assessment grid	25
Task 7	**Dim and Dimmer**	Teacher sheet	26
		Pupil sheet	27
		Assessment grid	28
Task 8	**Burger Chain**	Teacher sheet	30
		Pupil sheet	31
		Assessment grid	32
Task 9	**Dodgy Kebab**	Teacher sheet	33
		Pupil sheet	34
		Assessment grid	35
Task 10	**A Powdery Problem**	Teacher sheet	36
		Pupil sheet	37
		Assessment grid	38
Task 11	**Hotto Choco**	Teacher sheet	39
		Pupil sheet	40
		Assessment grid	41
Task 12	**Trapeze Trouble**	Teacher sheet	42
		Pupil sheet	43
		Assessment grid	44
Task 13	**Bella's Back Yard**	Teacher sheet	45
		Pupil sheet	46
		Assessment grid	47
Task 14	**Dodgem Newton**	Teacher sheet	48
		Pupil sheet	49
		Assessment grid	50

Introduction

APP for Science is designed to help you accurately assess your pupils' abilities using practical and research-based activities that are easy to use, understand and resource and which are fun for children to do. There is full curriculum coverage and support for ensuring skills progression.

What is Assessing Pupils' Progress for Primary Science (APP)?

APP is the new structured approach to teacher assessment, developed by the QCA in partnership with the DCFS, which helps teachers to make judgements on pupils' progress in Primary Science. It equips teachers with the tools to fine-tune their understanding of learners' needs and to tailor their planning and teaching accordingly. The aim is to provide a generalised agreement of pupil progress across the Primary phase to ensure skills progression into Key Stage 3.

APP is intended to be used as a periodic assessment of pupils through evidence collected of their work both written and otherwise.

The Assessment Foci

Pupils are assessed against five Assessment Foci (AFs). These are:

AF1: Thinking Scientifically. This focus involves children asking questions and understanding how science can answer such questions.

AF2: Understanding the Applications and Implications of Science. This focus looks at how children see science being used in their daily lives and draws on links between Science and Technology.

AF3: Communicating and Collaborating in Science. This focus concentrates on how children present their ideas about science, use scientific language and work together in a scientific context.

AF4: Using Investigative Approaches. This focus is on planning and doing investigations, collecting data and controlling risk.

AF5: Working Critically with Evidence. This focus concentrates on the thinking children have done in their investigations, what they found out and whether it was what they expected.

The benefits of APP

- Works together with Assessment for Learning strategies to help you learn more about pupils' strengths and weaknesses in science
- Helps you track pupil progress in science over time
- Allows you to make judgements about pupils' attainment linked to National Curriculum levels
- Provides a framework for you to share with pupils where they are and what they need to do to make progress
- Helps you in your curriculum planning and promotes teaching that is matched to pupil needs
- Helps you identify gaps in provision or areas that need review.

How to use this book

This book is intended to help you familiarise yourself with assessing the level of your pupils' work in real-life classroom practice in Primary Science. It is a book full of great ideas for investigations, and guidance notes and pointers on how children's responses to these investigations can inform your APP judgement.

APP Assessment Grid

At the beginning of this book we have provided a copy of the APP Assessment Foci Grid for Primary Science which comes from the DCSF. This assessment grid is designed to be photocopied and then highlighted so that following an assessment task you can level a child's work against each AF to see where they are at and what they need to do next to move up a level. It can then be used in subsequent assessment tasks to help you plot a child's progress and inform your future planning.

Tasks

There are 14 tasks which cover the second half of Key Stage 2 and are applicable to children in Year 5 and Year 6. We have linked task coverage to the National Curriculum Programme of Study and also to the QCA Scheme of Work. All the tasks cover Sc1 in the National Curriculum Programme of Study. Reference to Sc1 is mentioned on tasks where it is particularly relevant. However, each task can stand alone and there are also opportunities which are broad ranging and aimed at giving children the opportunity to conduct full investigations which are not directly linked to the QCA Scheme of Work. There are two of these longer investigations per book.

Teacher Sheets

Each task incorporates a Teacher Sheet offering an overview of the task, detailing resources needed, the key concepts it covers and giving advice and support for undertaking it. There are also suggestions for ways of approaching the tasks and on outcomes and recording which can be adapted by you to suit the needs of your class. Throughout the course of the 14 tasks you will have the opportunity to revisit each Assessment Focus several times and to focus on different statements within the AF more than once. We outlined two main Assessment Foci for the standard tasks and there are two tasks which cover all five of the AFs.

Pupil Sheets

Each task also incorporates a Pupil Sheet to put the task in a fun and motivational context, prompt children as they undertake the task and outline key vocabulary.

Assessment Sheets

We have taken the larger APP Assessment Foci Grid and broken it down into more specific Assessment Grids which are relevant to the tasks within the book. As each task covers two AFs we have adapted the Assessment Grids for these AFs and given specific examples of what a child might say or do to help you make level judgements more easily. These grids are also designed to be photocopied and highlighted and, where appropriate, examples of the child's work attached as evidence. This can be kept as part of an assessment portfolio.

We have made suggestions as to which AF you might like to focus on for each investigation but this is not obligatory. If we have suggested that a particular task is suitable for assessing 'planning' for example, but you feel you'd rather concentrate on 'drawing conclusions', then that's fine. The tasks are quite open ended and the focus can be easily changed. The grids cover National Curriculum Attainment Levels 3, 4 and 5 in all the Assessment Foci (AF1–AF5).

Using the Tasks

The tasks are linked in to the most widely used science topic areas of the National Curriculum in the second half of Key Stage 2. The majority of tasks are suitable for use near the end of a topic when children have acquired some knowledge of the topic content and they can all be integrated into your own school's science planning. NB: We expect that you will make an assessment of your children's learning before starting any of the tasks and adapt them accordingly so opportunities for class and group discussions are included. Children should not feel as if they are being 'tested' by these tasks, it is the intention that the tasks can be incorporated into your normal planning for science.

The tasks cover at least three levels (3–5) in at least two AFs. This does not mean that you have to assess every statement in those levels for the task, only those you choose to focus on.

The tasks are designed to be completed within a morning or afternoon session although those tasks which involve observing and measuring over time (growing plants for example) will take longer.

You'll notice too that the tasks also provide opportunities to record or develop skills in literacy and mathematics and can be used as assessment opportunities for APP in those subjects too.

Working out a Level

We have designed the tasks to be teacher assessed as APP is a tool for teachers rather than a self review tool for children. However, you may wish to share Success Criteria with the children and we have given guidance on question prompts and discussion points within the teacher pages.

Within the task-specific assessment grids, we have provided level descriptors and detailed level progression across three levels for each of the featured AFs. Instead of only giving generalised statements, we have also provided examples of how certain statements can be demonstrated. NB: Due to the open nature of APP there will be more than one way of demonstrating each statement.

When a pupil satisfies the criteria for a particular level statement within a particular Assessment Focus, it provides evidence that the child is working at that level. The child does not need to satisfy all of the AF statements at that level to qualify as working securely within it.

Over the final two years of Key Stage 2, children will produce a lot of work that can be assessed using the APP criteria and if a child is consistently satisfying statements within a particular level then that provides you with evidence that the pupil is working securely at this level.

Three reviews per year are recommended, and by incorporating some or all of these fourteen fun and engaging tasks into your science planning you will have a multitude of sound, reliable and realistic opportunities for assessing pupil's progress in science.

APP Primary Science Assessment Guidelines: levels 1 and 2

	AF1 – Thinking scientifically	AF2 – Understanding the applications and implications of science	AF3 – Communicating and collaborating in science	AF4 – Using investigative approaches	AF5 – Working critically with evidence
L1	**Across a range of contexts and practical situations pupils:** • Ask questions stimulated by their exploration of their world • Recognise basic features of objects, living things or events • Draw on their everyday experience to help answer questions • Respond to suggestions to identify some evidence (in the form of information, observations or measurements) that has been used to answer a question	**Across a range of contexts and practical situations pupils:** • Identify a link to science in familiar objects or contexts • Recognise scientific and technological developments that help us	**Across a range of contexts and practical situations pupils:** • Use everyday terms to describe simple features or actions of objects, living things or events they observe • Present evidence they have collected in simple templates provided for them • Communicate simple features or components of objects, living things or events they have observed in appropriate forms • Share their own ideas and listen to the ideas of others	**Across a range of contexts and practical situations pupils:** • Respond to prompts by making some simple suggestions about how to find an answer or make observations • Use their senses and simple equipment to make observations	**Across a range of contexts and practical situations pupils:** • Respond to prompts to say what happened • Say what has changed when observing objects, living things or events
L2	**Across a range of contexts and practical situations pupils:** • Draw on their observations and ideas to offer answers to questions • Make comparisons between basic features or components of objects, living things or events • Sort and group objects, living things or events on the basis of what they have observed • Respond to suggestions to identify some evidence (in the form of information, observations or measurements) needed	**Across a range of contexts and practical situations pupils:** • Express personal feelings or opinions about scientific or technological phenomena • Describe, in familiar contexts, how science helps people do things • Identify people who use science to help others • Identify scientific or technological phenomena and say whether or not they are helpful	**Across a range of contexts and practical situations pupils:** • Present their ideas and evidence in appropriate ways • Respond to prompts by using simple texts and electronic media to find information • Use simple scientific vocabulary to describe their ideas and observations • Work together on an experiment or investigation and recognise contributions made by others	**Across a range of contexts and practical situations pupils:** • Make some suggestions about how to find things out or how to collect data to answer a question or idea they are investigating • Identify things to measure or observe that are relevant to the question or idea they are investigating • Correctly use equipment provided to make observations and measurements • Make measurements, using standard or non-standard units as appropriate	**Across a range of contexts and practical situations pupils:** • Say what happened in their experiment or investigation • Say whether what happened was what they expected, acknowledging any unexpected outcomes • Respond to prompts to suggest different ways they could have done things
BL					
IE					

Overall assessment (tick one box only)   Low 1 ☐   Secure 1 ☐   High 1 ☐   Low 2 ☐   Secure 2 ☐   High 2 ☐

BL = 'Below Level'   IE = 'Insufficient Evidence'

APP Primary Science Assessment Guidelines: levels 3 and 4

	AF1 – Thinking scientifically	AF2 – Understanding the applications and implications of science	AF3 – Communicating and collaborating in science	AF4 – Using investigative approaches	AF5 – Working critically with evidence
L3	**Across a range of contexts and practical situations pupils:** • Identify differences, similarities or changes related to simple scientific ideas, processes or phenomena • Respond to ideas given to them to answer questions or suggest solutions to problems • Represent things in the real world using simple physical models • Use straightforward scientific evidence to answer questions, or to support their findings	**Across a range of contexts and practical situations pupils:** • Explain the purposes of a variety of scientific or technological developments • Link applications to specific characteristics or properties • Identify aspects of our lives, or of the work that people do, which are based on scientific ideas	**Across a range of contexts and practical situations pupils:** • Present simple scientific data in more than one way, including tables and bar charts • Use scientific forms of language when communicating simple scientific ideas, processes or phenomena • Identify simple advantages of working together on experiments or investigations	**Across a range of contexts and practical situations pupils:** • Identify one or more control variables in investigations from those provided • Select equipment or information sources from those provided to address a question or idea under investigation • Make some accurate observations or whole number measurements relevant to questions or ideas under investigation • Recognise obvious risks when prompted	**Across a range of contexts and practical situations pupils:** • Identify straightforward patterns in observations or in data presented in various formats, including tables, pie and bar charts • Describe what they have found out in experiments or investigations, linking cause and effect • Suggest improvements to their working methods
L4	**Across a range of contexts and practical situations pupils:** • Use scientific ideas when describing simple processes or phenomena • Use simple models to describe scientific ideas • Identify scientific evidence that is being used to support or refute ideas or arguments	**Across a range of contexts and practical situations pupils:** • Describe some simple positive and negative consequences of scientific and technological developments • Recognise applications of specific scientific ideas • Identify aspects of science used within particular jobs or roles	**Across a range of contexts and practical situations pupils:** • Select appropriate ways of presenting scientific data • Use appropriate scientific forms of language to communicate scientific ideas, processes or phenomena • Use scientific and mathematical conventions when communicating information or ideas	**Across a range of contexts and practical situations pupils:** • Decide when it is appropriate to carry out fair tests in investigations • Select appropriate equipment or information sources to address specific questions or ideas under investigation • Make sets of observations or measurements, identifying the ranges and intervals used • Identify possible risks to themselves and others	**Across a range of contexts and practical situations pupils:** • Identify patterns in data presented in various formats, including line graphs • Draw straightforward conclusions from data presented in various formats • Identify scientific evidence they have used in drawing conclusions • Suggest improvements to their working methods, giving reasons
BL					
IE					

Overall assessment (tick one box only)   Low 3 ☐   Secure 3 ☐   High 3 ☐   Low 4 ☐   Secure 4 ☐   High 4 ☐   BL = 'Below Level'   IE = 'Insufficient Evidence'

APP Primary Science Assessment Guidelines: Levels 5 and 6

	AF1 – Thinking scientifically	AF2 – Understanding the applications and implications of science	AF3 – Communicating and collaborating in science	AF4 – Using investigative approaches	AF5 – Working critically with evidence
L5	**Across a range of contexts and practical situations pupils:** • Use abstract ideas or models or more than one step when describing processes or phenomena • Explain processes or phenomena, suggest solutions to problems or answer questions by drawing on abstract ideas or models • Recognise scientific questions that do not have definitive answers • Identify the use of evidence and creative thinking by scientists in the development of scientific ideas	**Across a range of contexts and practical situations pupils:** • Describe different viewpoints a range of people may have about scientific or technological developments • Indicate how scientific or technological developments may affect different groups of people in different ways • Identify ethical or moral issues linked to scientific or technological developments • Link applications of science or technology to their underpinning scientific ideas	**Across a range of contexts and practical situations pupils:** • Distinguish between opinion and scientific evidence in contexts related to science, and use evidence rather than opinion to support or challenge scientific arguments • Decide on the most appropriate formats to present sets of scientific data, such as using line graphs for continuous variables • Use appropriate scientific and mathematical conventions and terminology to communicate abstract ideas • Suggest how collaborative approaches to specific experiments or investigations may improve the evidence collected	**Across a range of contexts and practical situations pupils:** • Recognise significant variables in investigations, selecting the most suitable to investigate • Explain why particular pieces of equipment or information sources are appropriate for the questions or ideas under investigation • Repeat sets of observations or measurements where appropriate, selecting suitable ranges and intervals • Make, and act on, suggestions to control obvious risks to themselves and others	**Across a range of contexts and practical situations pupils:** • Interpret data in a variety of formats, recognising obvious inconsistencies • Provide straightforward explanations for differences in repeated observations or measurements • Draw valid conclusions that utilise more than one piece of supporting evidence, including numerical data and line graphs • Evaluate the effectiveness of their working methods, making practical suggestions for improving them
L6	**Across a range of contexts and practical situations pupils:** • Use abstract ideas or models or multiple factors when explaining processes or phenomena • Identify the strengths and weaknesses of particular models • Describe some scientific evidence that supports or refutes particular ideas or arguments, including those in development • Explain how new scientific evidence is discussed and interpreted by the scientific community and how this may lead to changes in scientific ideas	**Across a range of contexts and practical situations pupils:** • Describe how different decisions on the uses of scientific and technological developments may be made in different economic, social or cultural contexts • Explain how societies are affected by particular scientific applications or ideas • Describe how particular scientific or technological developments have provided evidence to help scientists pose and answer further questions • Describe how aspects of science are applied in particular jobs or roles	**Across a range of contexts and practical situations pupils:** • Identify lack of balance in the presentation of information or evidence • Choose forms to communicate qualitative or quantitative data appropriate to the data and the purpose of the communication • Distinguish between data and information from primary sources, secondary sources and simulations, and present them in the most appropriate form	**Across a range of contexts and practical situations pupils:** • Apply scientific knowledge and understanding in the planning of investigations, identifying significant variables and recognising which are independent and which are dependent • Justify their choices of data collection method and proposed number of observations and measurements • Collect data choosing appropriate ranges, numbers and values for measurements and observations • Independently recognise a range of familiar risks and take action to control them	**Across a range of contexts and practical situations pupils:** • Suggest reasons based on scientific knowledge and understanding for any limitations or inconsistencies in evidence collected • Select and manipulate data and information and use them to contribute to conclusions • Draw conclusions that are consistent with the evidence they have collected and explain them using scientific knowledge and understanding • Make valid comments on the quality of their data
BL					
IE					

Overall assessment (tick one box only)   Low 5 ☐   Secure 5 ☐   High 5 ☐   Low 6 ☐   Secure 6 ☐   High 6 ☐   BL = 'Below Level'   IE = 'Insufficient Evidence'

Task 1 Ready, Steady Scoff!

APP	National Curriculum Programme of Study: Sc2 2b,g,h	Resources
AF1		• two plastic carrier bags with following contents (real ingredients are preferable but pictures would do)
AF4	QCA Scheme of Work: 5a	

National Curriculum Programme of Study: Sc2 2b,g,h

QCA Scheme of Work: 5a

Resources

• two plastic carrier bags with following contents (real ingredients are preferable but pictures would do)

Bag 1:
- o sugar cubes
- o potatoes
- o pasta
- o butter
- o double cream

Bag 2:
- o chicken
- o green beans
- o tomatoes
- o brown rice

• access to Internet
• Task 1 Pupil Sheets

Task overview

Research-based investigation using secondary sources to debate a question on a balanced diet and healthy living.

Key concepts

• Balanced diet
• Keeping healthy

Outcomes

• Children prepare an email to a television producer explaining what makes a balanced diet and healthy lifestyle.

Teaching notes

• Set the scene for the task by discussing whether children have watched television programmes like the one described on the Pupil Sheet. Discuss the contents of the two shopping bags. *Was Rick Stone right to feel cheated?*

• Review children's knowledge of food groups and what is meant by a balanced diet, e.g. *Can we never eat chocolate?* Explain the terms 'in moderation' as related to diet.

• *Is 'What is a good diet to promote good health?' a question we can answer by experimenting in the classroom? For example, can we feed half the class items from bag one for a year and the other half items from bag two – is that sensible? How can we find the information we need?* Suggest research on the Internet or in libraries or ask an expert.

• Look at reputable Internet sites on diet and health. Discuss where we might find information and which sites to trust e.g. professional associations rather than commercial food producers who are trying to market a product.

• Children investigate diet and health using various sources of information.

• Children use the information they have discovered to back up their arguments to the television company. They can also include information on other aspects of healthy lifestyles including avoidance of tobacco products, harmful effects of illegal drug taking, moderation in alcohol consumption and taking regular exercise.

Task 1 Ready, Steady Scoff!

In the tv programme *Ready, Steady Scoff!* top chefs compete to create a balanced meal from ingredients provided by the audience. Rick Stone was downcast having lost with sugar cubes, bread rolls, butter, potatoes, pasta and double cream. 'There was no way I could have won with those ingredients,' he complained.

Winner, Johnny Oliver, who was given chicken, green beans, tomatoes and brown rice said, 'Rick's just being a bad loser. The best chef won!'

Who do you think is right?

What you need to do

Write an email to the producers of *Ready, Steady, Scoff!* explaining:

• what a balanced diet is and what we need to eat to keep healthy

• what advice the producers of the show should give to the audience about selecting foods for the chefs to cook

• what else we should all be doing to keep healthy.

You may find these words helpful

carbohydrate, protein, fats, vegetables, balance, exercise, moderate, moderation

Task 1 Ready, Steady Scoff!

	Level 3 Across a range of contexts and practical situations pupils:	Level 4 Across a range of contexts and practical situations pupils:	Level 5 Across a range of contexts and practical situations pupils:
AF1 Thinking scientifically	• Respond to ideas given to them to answer questions or suggest solutions to problems **e.g. can recognise forms of information other than first hand evidence can help answer a science question** • Represent things in the real world using simple physical models **e.g. can create a balanced 'lunch box' meal using representations of food and/or food groups**	• Use simple models to describe scientific ideas **e.g. uses 'the plate of good health' as a representation of balance in a diet** • Identify scientific evidence that is being used to support or refute ideas or arguments **e.g. I know that scientists have found that eating too much fat and sugar can make you overweight and that this might harm your health.**	• Use abstract ideas or models or more than one step when describing processes/phenomena **e.g. knows that different food groups or a balance of elements in a healthy lifestyle (e.g. exercise, not taking drugs) are important for good health for different reasons** • Recognise scientific questions that do not yet have definitive answers **e.g. knows that views about diet and health have changed over time and that they may change again**
AF4 Using investigative approaches	• Select equipment or information sources from those provided to address a question or idea under investigation **e.g. can use references in books or on the internet about healthy living** • Make some accurate observations or whole number measurements relevant to questions or ideas under investigation **e.g. can sort foods into food groups**	• Select appropriate equipment or information sources to address specific questions or ideas under investigation **e.g. can find references in books or on the internet about healthy living and make a choice about how trustworthy or accurate the sources of information may be** • Make sets of observations or measurements, identifying the ranges and intervals used **e.g. can identify some foods which are high in fat and others which have little fat content**	• Explain why particular pieces of equipment or information sources are appropriate for the questions or ideas under investigation **e.g. can understand that all information presented may not be true or of equal value. Begins to understand opinion and bias in reporting** • Repeat sets of observations or measurements where appropriate, selecting suitable ranges and intervals **e.g. can compare different diets and suggest modifications to content to make them healthier e.g. The contents of bag 'A' contained no green vegetables or protein so were less balanced than bag 'B'.**

Task 2 Seed Triathlon

APP	**National Curriculum Programme of Study:** Sc2 3d 5b,c
AF4	**QCA Scheme of Work:** 5b
AF5	

Task overview

Investigation into seed design and methods of dispersal.

Key concepts

• seed dispersal
• plant life cycles
• comparing
• collecting data
• accurate measuring

Outcomes

• Children prepare a report and then take part in a debate deciding which seed should be awarded the title 'Seed Triathlon Champion'.

Resources

• selection of seeds which are dispersed in different ways e.g. sycamore, pine cones, apple or berries, coconut, burdock, acorns, beans, etc
• selection of modelling materials to make model seeds, e.g. confetti, balloons, paper spinners
• measuring tapes
• ICT data loggers
• water troughs
• Task 2 Pupil Sheets

Teaching notes

• Review children's knowledge on plant life cycles and in particular the ways in which seeds from the parent plant are dispersed.

• Set the scene for the task by introducing the idea of a triathlon – do children know what it is? *It is a three part race where competitors swim, cycle and run over a long distance.* Explain that they are going to try a 'seed triathlon' and test a selection of seeds over three methods of dispersal. *How well will the seeds perform in the air, through water and over land? In each case we want to look at the furthest distance the seeds can travel from the source.* You may want to time limit this.

• Children can use models (e.g. paper spinners, balloons filled with confetti, etc) or real seeds. The emphasis here is on accurate measuring, recognising where comparisons are incomplete and where data cannot be directly compared.

• Children can nominate which seeds they want to investigate and how they will conduct their tests; each group can do something different.

• It may be helpful to have access to the outdoors to carry out the tests. If you have a sloping field then children can test which seeds roll down the slope furthest. ICT data loggers work well here to measure speed of travel down a slope.

• After children have completed their tests they can report back verbally to the other groups on what they discovered and which seeds they'll nominate either as overall winner or highly commended in each category. If there is disagreement then children can debate their points of evidence and take a vote.

Task 2 Seed Triathlon

'And here we are at the start of the seed triathlon. Which seeds will survive through wind, water and over land and take the ultimate prize?'

Can you find out which seed will win?

What you need to do

• In groups plan a seed triathlon to test which seed is the best at dispersing by air or wind, across water, and over land. Is there one seed that is good at all three? Use real seeds or make models.

• Report your findings to the rest of your class. Does everyone agree? Be prepared to argue the case for your seed triathlon champion!

You may find these words helpful

disperse, dispersal, wind, water, explosion, animal, model

Task 2 Seed Triathlon

	Level 3 Across a range of contexts and practical situations pupils:	Level 4 Across a range of contexts and practical situations pupils:	Level 5 Across a range of contexts and practical situations pupils:
AF4 **Using Investigative Approaches**	• Select equipment or information sources from those provided to address a question or idea under investigation **e.g. can choose sensible measuring equipment for distance from a selection such as a tape measure with cm scale** • Make some accurate observations or whole number measurements relevant to questions or ideas under investigation **e.g. The pine cone travelled 340 cm.**	• Select appropriate equipment or information sources to address specific questions or ideas under investigation **e.g. can ask for a tape measure or a metre rule which measures cm** • Make sets of observations or measurements, identifying the ranges and intervals used **e.g. We measured in centimetres and rounded up to the nearest 10cm. The shortest distance was 300cms and the longest 460cms.**	• Explain why particular pieces of equipment or information sources are appropriate for the questions or ideas under investigation **e.g. can select a tape measure rather than a metre rule because it will be more accurate when measuring distances over one metre** • Repeat sets of observations or measurements where appropriate, selecting suitable ranges and intervals **e.g. We repeated each measurement three times and took an average. The average distance the pine cone travelled was 367cms; the shortest distance was 308cms and the longest 463cms.**
AF5 **Working Critically with Evidence**	• Describe what they have found out in experiments or investigations, linking cause and effect **e.g. can identify a 'winning' seed that travelled the furthest distance by one dispersal method** • Suggest improvements to their working methods **e.g. recognises that some measurements may not be accurate or that conditions e.g. wind blowing, may influence the reliability of the test**	• Identify scientific evidence they have used in drawing conclusions **e.g. can identify the 'winning' seeds for each method of dispersal by stating the distances travelled** • Suggest improvements to their working methods, giving reasons **e.g. suggests making more than one test and repeating measurements to be sure of the results**	• Draw valid conclusions that utilise more than one piece of supporting evidence, including numerical data and line graphs **e.g. can identify a 'winning' seed by finding the highest average for all three methods of dispersal** • Evaluate the effectiveness of their working methods, making practical suggestions for improving them **e.g. recognises the drawbacks in their testing methods and makes realistic attempts to control for these such as doing all tests indoors**

Task 3 A Lighter Loaf

APP	National Curriculum Programme of Study: Sc2 5f Sc3 1e, 2a,f
AF4	QCA Scheme of Work: 5c
AF5	

Task overview
Children plan a fair test to investigate how the amount of sugar affects carbon dioxide production when added to yeast.

Key concepts
• Planning a fair test
• Use of gases

Outcomes
• Children write instructions to Mrs Rose on how to carry out a fair test to solve her problem.

Resources
• yeast – dried or fresh
• sugar
• warm water
• thermometer
• measuring cylinders or graduated beakers
• spoons
• digital scales
• test tubes or thin measuring cylinders
• balloons small enough to fit over top of test tube
• Task 3 Pupil Sheets

Teaching notes
• We are focussing on planning in this task although you may choose to let children complete the full investigation.

• Set the scene for the task by explaining that yeast is fungus, a single-celled microorganism which uses sugar for living and growth. When warm water is added it activates the yeast which begins feeding on the sugar. As a result of this, carbon dioxide is released and when the bubbles of carbon dioxide get trapped in bread dough they help the bread to rise making it light.

• Allow children time in their groups to discuss how they will plan and conduct their investigation.

• Bring the discussion back to the whole class and ask them what they will do and how they will measure the amount of carbon dioxide released. Discuss how a balloon attached to the top of the test tube/measuring cylinder will fill with any carbon dioxide released.

• Ask children how they will make their investigation fair and which variables they have identified. The amount of sugar is the change variable – which others do they need to keep the same? How will they measure the sugar? Which equipment will they use? (e.g. measuring cylinders, thermometers/ digital scales)

• Once planned, children write a short set of instructions to Mrs Rose on how to carry out the test.

Task 3 A Lighter Loaf

Mrs Rose wants to enter the Baker of the Year competition and beat her rival baker, Mr White, who makes a very light loaf.

Mrs Rose thinks if she can make yeast produce more gas then there will be more bubbles which will make her bread lighter than Mr White's.

Can you help Mrs Rose increase the amount of gas the yeast produces?

What you need to do

• Write a set of instructions for Mrs Rose explaining how she could investigate the problem by carrying out a fair test.

• Explain which variables she needs to change and which she needs to keep the same.

You may find these words helpful

gas, carbon dioxide, volume, fair test, variable, change, control, measure, compare, because

Task 3 A Lighter Loaf

	Level 3 — Across a range of contexts and practical situations pupils:	Level 4 — Across a range of contexts and practical situations pupils:	Level 5 — Across a range of contexts and practical situations pupils:
AF4 Using investigative approaches	• Identify one or more control variables in investigations from those provided **e.g. can identify volume or heat of water as variables to be controlled** • Make some accurate observations or whole number measurements relevant to questions or ideas under investigation **e.g. can state through observation which balloon was the biggest**	• Decide when it is appropriate to carry out fair tests in investigations **e.g. can explain why they are only changing one variable** • Make sets of observations or measurements, identifying the ranges and intervals used **e.g. can state through observation which balloon was the biggest and can identify the optimum amount of sugar or heat**	• Recognise significant variables in investigations, selecting the most suitable to investigate **e.g. is able to identify amount of sugar or heat of water as a variable and conduct investigation into one of their own choice** • Repeat sets of observations or measurements where appropriate, selecting suitable ranges and intervals **e.g. is aware that validity of results can be improved by repeating observations**
AF5 Working critically with evidence	• Identify straightforward patterns in observations or in data presented in various formats, including tables, pie and bar charts **e.g. The test tube with x amount of sugar had the biggest balloon.** • Describe what they have found out in experiments or investigations, linking cause and effect **e.g. The balloon on test tube x was the biggest.**	• Identify patterns in data presented in various formats, including line graphs **e.g. The more sugar we used the bigger the balloon expanded.** • Draw straightforward conclusions from data presented in various formats **e.g. The balloon attached to test tube x expanded the most. This means that most carbon dioxide was produced in this tube.**	• Interpret data in a variety of formats, recognising obvious inconsistencies **e.g. I knew that I needed to check the validity of our results by repeating the experiment.** • Provide straightforward explanations for differences in repeated observations or measurements **e.g can recognise that there may be difference in the results of their repeat readings due to human error**

© Pearson Education Ltd 2010. APP for Science Years 5 and 6

Task 4 Soggy Socks

APP	National Curriculum Programme of Study: Sc1 1a, 2c,k,l Sc3 2e
AF1	QCA Scheme of Work: 5d
AF5	

Task overview
Children solve the problem of how to dry damp socks quickly.

Key concepts
• Evaporation of liquids
• Problem solving
• Use of evidence to support or refute ideas

Outcomes
• Children write explanation to the Foundation teacher explaining how the socks were dried and why it worked and where the water went.

Resources
• damp small children's-sized socks
• washing line put up both inside and outside
• pegs
• radiators with thermostats (if possible)
• fans and hairdryers if they have been tested for electrical safety
• damp meter (if available)
• digital balance
• thermometers
• Post-it notes
• sandwich bags
• Task 4 Pupil Sheets

Teaching notes
• You may want to pick a dry windy day to carry out this assessment.

• Set the scene for the task by telling children that some of the Reception children have been splashing in a puddle at lunch time and have ended up with soggy socks. Their teacher has wrung them out and patted them with a towel but they are still not completely dry. She is now wondering how to get them dry before the children go home and whether you can help to make sure they don't go home with cold damp feet.

• Talk to children about when they have seen puddles 'dry up' quickly and how they get things dry at home. Encourage them to come up with examples such as *wet hair dries quicker using a hairdryer* as do wet clothes put out on the line in the sun and wind or in the tumble drier.

• Get each child to write a note on a large Post-it note about what they would do to get the socks dry, why they think it will work and what they think happens to the water.

• When they have had a chance to formulate their ideas put them into groups where they decide on a group approach to drying the socks. Give each group a sandwich bag with a pair of damp, clean, small socks in it.

• Keep one pair in a bag as a control if you want to compare what happens when no extra heat or moving air is available to the socks. If you are weighing the socks take a 'wet' weight measurement.

• Let children try out their plans and then at the end of the afternoon measure damp levels remaining with a damp meter or weigh the dry socks and find the difference in weight to establish how much water has evaporated or touch test the socks.

• **Keep Safe! Do not put socks directly over the end of a hairdryer.**

• Discuss which was the most effective method and why.

• Tell children they are going to return the socks but they also need to enclose a note explaining how they dried the socks and what has happened to the water.

Task 4 Soggy Socks

Some of the children in Reception have been playing in puddles at lunch time and have made their socks wet.

Their teacher would like your help to get them dry before the children go home.

Can you help the teacher dry the socks and explain to the children where the water goes?

What you need to do

• In a group decide how you are going to best dry the socks.

• When the socks are dry, write a note to the Reception children and their teacher explaining how you dried the socks and where the water has gone.

You may find these words helpful

damp, dry, evaporate, evaporation, quickly, quickest, because

© Pearson Education Ltd 2010. APP for Science Years 5 and 6

Task 4 Soggy Socks

	Level 3	Level 4	Level 5
AF1 Thinking scientifically	**Across a range of contexts and practical situations pupils:** • Respond to ideas given to them to answer questions or suggest solutions to problems **e.g. can assess the usefulness or otherwise of equipment at their disposal talks about other solutions e.g. Wouldn't it be great if we had a tumble drier?** • Use straightforward scientific evidence to answer questions, or to support their findings **e.g. can measure mass of sock to nearest gram**	**Across a range of contexts and practical situations pupils:** • Identify scientific evidence that is being used to support or refute ideas or arguments **e.g. We can tell that the water is evaporating faster when the temperature is higher.** • Identify scientific evidence that is being used to support or refute ideas or arguments **e.g. measures mass of sock at beginning and end of investigation and calculate the difference. Know the change in mass is the mass of evaporated water**	**Across a range of contexts and practical situations pupils:** • Recognise scientific questions that do not yet have definitive answers **e.g. Will we be able to find a way of drying clothes as quickly and efficiently as in a tumble drier without using electricity?** • Identify the use of evidence and creative thinking by scientists in the development of scientific ideas **e.g. calculates average loss of mass under different conditions and suggests whether this might lead to further investigations**
AF5 Working critically with evidence	• Identify straightforward patterns in observations or in data presented in various formats, including tables, pie and bar charts **e.g. identifies simple trend in results listing conditions from driest to wettest end result** • Describe what they have found out in experiments or investigations, linking cause and effect **e.g. describes what they did to get the socks to dry quicker and that warmth and/or wind dries things quicker**	• Identify patterns in data presented in various formats, including line graphs **e.g. suggests drawing graph with numerical values of loss of mass in grams** • Identify scientific evidence they have used in drawing conclusions **e.g. uses loss of mass in grams to conclude warmer and/or moving air speeds up evaporation**	• Interpret data in a variety of formats, recognising obvious inconsistencies **e.g. recognises values in data which do not fit the general trend as being inconsistent** • Draw valid conclusions that utilise more than one piece of supporting evidence, including numerical data and line graphs **e.g. draws on own and others results and concludes that warmer and moving air speeds up evaporation. Can relate speed of drying to temperature of environment**

Task 5 Out of this World!

APP AF1 AF2	**National Curriculum Programme of Study:** BoS 1b Sc4 4c **QCA Scheme of Work:** 5e

Task overview
Children consider purpose/ethics of space exploration. They find out why Earth has day and night.

Key concepts
• Application of science and technology
• Day and night
• Benefits and disadvantages

Outcomes
• Children write outline for blog about space exploration.
• They include an explanation of why Earth has day and night.

Resources
• research material on space exploration and Guy Laliberté
• access to Internet
• video/camera (optional)
• modelling materials
• Task 5 Pupil Sheets

Teaching notes

• Discuss why humans want to explore the Earth, extend to space exploration. Consider some benefits (extending experience and knowledge, spin-off advances in technology, etc) and disadvantages (expensive, dangerous, etc).

• Ask children to browse research material to extend knowledge of space.

• Set the scene for the task by discussing Guy Laliberté, the first clown in space. He wanted to entertain people and at the same time communicate a serious worldwide message. View his video blog which was the first from the International Space Station on the Internet. Go to **www.pearsonhotlinks.co.uk**, search for APP for Science and click on this activity.

• Discuss how people have seen Earth from the International Space Station. *What does it look like?* People can see that the side of the Earth which faces the Sun is illuminated and experiences daytime. They can also see the change to night time as the Earth spins about its axis.

• Ask children to write a short blog considering the benefits and disadvantages of space exploration. Include an explanation on why Earth has day and night. They could communicate this by using models, singing, drawing cartoons, acting, etc.

• Evidence could be videoed, photographed or written.

Task 5 Out of this World!

In 2009, Canadian circus owner, Guy Laliberté became the first clown to orbit the Earth and to visit the International Space Station (ISS). He carried out the first video blog from space.

What would you say in a video blog from space?

What you need to do

- Carry out some research then write an outline for your video blog.
- Include:
  - your opinions about the good and bad points of space exploration
  - an explanation of why the Earth has day and night.

You may find these words helpful

day, night, spin, rotate, axis, benefits, disadvantages

Task 5 Out of this World!

	Level 3 Across a range of contexts and practical situations pupils:	Level 4 Across a range of contexts and practical situations pupils:	Level 5 Across a range of contexts and practical situations pupils:
AF1 Thinking scientifically	• Represent things in the real world using simple physical models **e.g. uses a sphere and light source to show that side facing light source has daytime** • Use straightforward scientific evidence to answer questions, or to support their findings **e.g. The light side of the Earth has daytime.**	• Use simple models to describe scientific ideas **e.g. uses rotating sphere and light source to model change of day to night** • Identify scientific evidence that is being used to support or refute ideas or arguments **e.g. We know the Earth spins because astronauts can see this.**	• Use abstract ideas or models or more than one step when describing processes or phenomena **e.g. uses diagrams and models to show how day and night is a consequence of Earth's rotation about its axis** • Identify the use of evidence and creative thinking by scientists in the development of scientific ideas **e.g. People used to believe that the Sun moves but now know that the same effect is given when the Earth spins; can describe the significance of Copernicus' ideas**
AF2 Understanding the applications and implications of science	• Explain the purposes of a variety of scientific or technological developments **e.g. Astronauts need spacesuits to help them stay alive.** • Identify aspects of our lives, or of the work that people do, which are based on scientific ideas **e.g. understands that our lives are governed by day and night**	• Describe some simple positive and negative consequences of scientific and technological developments **e.g. recognises that a lot of useful inventions have come from space technology, but it is very expensive** • Identify aspects of science used within particular jobs or roles **e.g. The International Space Station must keep the air inside so astronauts can breathe.**	• Describe different viewpoints a range of people may have about scientific or technological developments **e.g. recognises that some people think it is important to explore space, but others think it is not necessary** • Identify ethical or moral issues linked to scientific or technological developments **e.g. It costs a lot of money to go into space. This could be used to help ill or poor people.**

Task 6 Good Vibrations

APP	National Curriculum Programme of Study: Sc4 3e,f,g
AF2	QCA Scheme of Work: 5f
AF3	

Task overview

Investigation on changing the pitch of musical notes.

Key concepts

- How sounds are produced and travel
- Changing pitch

Outcomes

- Children compose and play a short musical piece.
- They provide a commentary describing why the sounds have changed pitch and how sound travels.

Resources

- selection of musical instruments – including pitched and unpitched
- metal dustbin lid
- soft topped drum beater
- tuning forks
- bowl of water
- balloons
- sound meter or data logger
- video camera
- Task 6 Pupil Sheets

Teaching notes

- Review the idea that pitch is a description of how high or low a sound is and that sounds are produced by making something vibrate. Demonstrate this using a tuning fork to produce vibrations on the surface of water that children can see or set the fork vibrating then gently stroke it across a balloon placed on a child's cheek so they can feel the vibrations.

- **Keep safe! Don't overinflate the balloon: it could burst.**

- Sometimes we can see vibrations, often we can't, but we can feel vibrations, particularly from very low sounds. *Have you ever stood on the pavement when a big lorry is going past and as well as hearing the noise you felt the vibrations?* You can replicate this by standing a child in front of a metal dustbin lid so that you are holding it with the round surface close but not touching the child's stomach. Gently strike the lid with the padded beater. They should feel vibrations in their body!

- Set the scene for the task by talking about Evelyn Glennie and how she 'hears' the music she plays even though she is deaf. Tell children they are going to compose some music with high and low pitched sounds in it. They must be able to commentate on their piece describing how the sounds are made and explaining why the pitch is either high or low.

- Let children investigate how to change the pitch of a selection of instruments. Try to include stringed and wind instruments as well as percussion. Can children come up with general rules about changing sounds? E.g. *the tighter the string the higher the note* or *the shorter the air column the higher the pitch*, etc.

- Children should consider how they can record pitch. How will they know if one sound is lower than another and by how much? You can use data loggers if you are able.

- Finally, children compose a short piece of music, which can be filmed or recorded, and commentate on how the sounds have been made, why the pitch has changed and how sound travels.

Task 6 Good Vibrations

Good Vibrations is the title of Scottish musician Dame Evelyn Glennie's autobiography. She is a world class solo percussionist. Glennie is also deaf and has been since she was 12 years old. She regularly plays in bare feet so that she can 'feel' the music.

She has written about sound being 'vibrating air'.

Can you find out how musical instruments make sounds?

What you need to do

• Investigate how sounds change.

• Compose or play a short piece of music which uses high and low sounds.

• Give a talk on how the sounds are produced and how the sound travels.

You may find these words helpful

vibrate, vibration, travel, wave, air, percussion, strings, tension, pitch, tuning

Task 6 Good Vibrations

	Level 3	Level 4	Level 5
AF2 **Understanding the applications and implications of science**	Across a range of contexts and practical situations pupils: • Explain the purposes of a variety of scientific or technological developments **e.g. Some deaf people use hearing aids to improve their hearing.** • Identify aspects of our lives, or of the work that people do, which are based on scientific ideas **e.g. Musicians need to recognise differently pitched notes to keep in tune.**	Across a range of contexts and practical situations pupils: • Describe some simple positive and negative consequences of scientific and technological developments **e.g. High pitched and discordant burglar alarms are good at attracting attention but are annoying if they go on too long.** • Identify aspects of science used within particular jobs or roles **e.g. Sometimes musicians need to alter the pitch of their instruments to keep in tune with the rest of the orchestra.**	Across a range of contexts and practical situations pupils: • Identify ethical or moral issues linked to scientific or technological developments **e.g. discusses fairness of using 'mosquito' high pitched noise generation devices to drive away teenagers from shopping centres while older shoppers are unaffected** • Link applications of science or technology to their underpinning scientific ideas **e.g. identifies which part of the instrument vibrates to create a sound and can explain how to alter this in a rule**
AF3 **Communicating and collaborating in science**	• Present simple scientific data in more than one way, including tables and bar charts **e.g. can make some graphical representation of high and low pitch** • Use scientific forms of language when communicating simple scientific ideas, processes or phenomena **e.g. can distinguish between pitch and volume**	• Select appropriate ways of presenting scientific data **e.g. can represent change of string length in a table and make some scale of pitch. Can transfer this data to a graph in a logical way** • Use appropriate scientific forms of language to communicate scientific ideas, processes or phenomena **e.g. can use scientific words and ideas correctly when offering explanations e.g. vibration, frequency**	• Distinguish between opinion and scientific evidence in science contexts, and use evidence rather than opinion to support or challenge scientific arguments **e.g. knows that volume can accurately be measured and factually be reported using dB scale** • Decide on the most appropriate formats to present sets of scientific data, such as using line graphs for continuous variables **e.g. can use a data logger (or oscilloscope if provided) to create a line graph showing changes of sounds over time (volume or pitch depending on sophistication of equipment available)**

Task 7 Dim and Dimmer

APP	National Curriculum Programme of Study: Sc1 1a,b 2a–m Sc4 1a–c
AF1 AF2 AF3 AF4 AF5	QCA Scheme of Work: 6g

Task overview
Investigation to find out what affects the brightness of a bulb in a circuit.

Key concepts
• Accurate measuring
• Systematic recording
• Fair testing

Outcomes
• Children prepare a series of line graphs showing effect of different lengths of fuse wire on the brightness of a bulb in a circuit, different widths of wire and/or different types of resistor.

Resources
• computer/datalogger with light sensor
• fuse wire (nichrome)
• metre rule
• batteries
• bulbs
• connecting wire with crocodile clips
• copper wire
• graphite rods
• 60 cm long balsa wood board with screw at either end to hold the different wires (to change the length of the wire, move the crocodile clips along the wire)
• Task 7 Pupil Sheets

Teaching notes

• Set the scene for the task by discussing the possible lighting system in a doll's house and how a dimmer switch might be a good idea. Ask children how they think they can change the brightness of the bulb in a circuit. Accept suggestions for changing the number of cells or bulbs but probe for other variables to test.

• Ask groups to spend time planning their investigation – each group can do something different. What variable will they change? What are the variables they need to control? What will they measure or observe?

• **Keep safe! Thin wire in a circuit can get very hot. Make sure children know not to touch wire in a connected circuit and to wait for it to cool down before changing it.**

• If you do not have access to a light sensor, plan how to judge the brightness of the bulb. How many readings will children take? *Do we need to take a reading of the circuit with no test wire in it? Why?*

• Give children access to a range of equipment and let them choose what they will need.

• Encourage systematic recording of their results, first in a table and then using the data logger to produce a line graph or have children draw one if they are able.

• Can children explain what is happening to the current in the circuit and why the bulb grows dimmer? Draw a circuit diagram as part of the explanation.

• Discuss other household appliances where we need to vary the output e.g. volume controls on radios.

Task 7   Dim and Dimmer

The after school club has been a bit rough with the new doll's house and have broken the light switch. The science club are trying to fix it for them.

Anna thinks they could improve the doll's house by adding a dimmer switch but she's not sure how dimmer switches work. Adam thinks it might be something to do with the length of the wire in the circuit that changes the brightness of the bulb. Sabina thinks it's something to do with the thickness of wire.

Can you help investigate?

What you need to do

- In groups test to see if the length or thickness of the wire in a circuit affects the brightness of the bulb.
- Draw your circuit diagram and make a graph of your results.

You may find these words helpful

circuit, nichrome wire, battery, cell, circuit diagram, resistance, variable resistor, component

Task 7 Dim and Dimmer

	Level 3 Across a range of contexts and practical situations pupils:	Level 4 Across a range of contexts and practical situations pupils:	Level 5 Across a range of contexts and practical situations pupils:
AF1 **Thinking Scientifically**	• Respond to ideas given to them to answer questions or suggest solutions to problems **e.g. We could make a circuit to test different thicknesses of wire and see how the bulb brightness changes.** • Use straightforward scientific evidence to answer questions, or to support their findings **e.g. can measure brightness using a sensor**	• Use scientific ideas when describing simple processes or phenomena **e.g. The bulb brightness changes because there is a different amount of electricity going through it.** • Identify scientific evidence that is being used to support or refute ideas or arguments **e.g. We'll accurately measure the brightness using a light sensor then we can be sure of how the brightness has changed.**	• Use abstract ideas or models or more than one step when describing processes or phenomena **e.g. Different thicknesses of wires must affect how much electricity flows because the bulb brightness changes.** • Identify the use of evidence and creative thinking by scientists in the development of scientific ideas **e.g. knows that dimmer switches used to work using simple variable resistors but now they are more sophisticated**
AF2 **Understanding the Applications and Implications of Science**	• Explain the purposes of a variety of scientific or technological developments **e.g. We need electricity to make our house lights work so we can see indoors at night.** • Link applications to specific characteristics or properties **e.g. understands that wires are made of metal because it conducts electricity**	• Describe some simple positive and negative consequences of scientific and technological developments **e.g. Electric lights are important because we need them in our houses at night, but the electricity costs money.** • Recognise applications of specific scientific ideas **e.g. We can change the brightness of the bulb by changing the length of wire in the circuit.**	• Indicate how scientific or technological developments may affect different groups of people in different ways **e.g. scientists are constantly trying to produce more energy efficient controllable lighting and to reduce costs** • Link applications of science or technology to their underpinning scientific ideas **e.g. New energy efficient bulbs waste less energy but older bulbs wasted a lot more heat energy.**

Task 7 Dim and Dimmer

	Level 3 Across a range of contexts and practical situations pupils:	Level 4 Across a range of contexts and practical situations pupils:	Level 5 Across a range of contexts and practical situations pupils:
AF3 **Communicating and Collaborating in Science**	• Present simple scientific data in more than one way, including tables and bar charts **e.g. produces two column table and circuit diagram** • Use scientific forms of language when communicating simple scientific ideas, processes or phenomena **e.g. Metal conducts electricity.**	• Select appropriate ways of presenting scientific data **e.g. uses line graph produced by data logger** • Use appropriate scientific forms of language to communicate scientific ideas, processes or phenomena **e.g. My diagram shows a complete circuit with symbols for each part.**	• Decide on the most appropriate formats to present sets of scientific data, such as using line graphs for continuous variables **e.g. can relate line graph from data logger to changing light levels over time** • Use appropriate scientific and mathematical conventions and terminology to communicate abstract ideas **e.g. My circuit diagram uses accurate electrical symbols for each component.**
AF4 **Using Investigative Approaches**	• Select equipment or information sources from those provided to address a question or idea under investigation **e.g. connects circuit accurately using equipment provided** • Recognise obvious risks when prompted **e.g. The thin wire gets hot so I must not touch it.**	• Select appropriate equipment or information sources to address specific questions or ideas under investigation **e.g. chooses to measure brightness using a sensor** • Identify possible risks to themselves and others **e.g. The thin wire gets warm and if it gets too hot, it could burn anyone who touches it.**	• Explain why particular pieces of equipment or information sources are appropriate for the questions or ideas under investigation **e.g. knows that gold and silver are good conductors but are too expensive for domestic wires** • Make, and act on, suggestions to control obvious risks to themselves and others **e.g. We will have a safety monitor to check that everyone has their hands away from the circuit before we switch it on.**
AF5 **Working Critically with Evidence**	• Identify straightforward patterns in observations or in data presented in various formats, including tables, pie and bar charts **e.g. We can see from the table that the longest wire gave the dimmest light.** • Describe what they have found out in experiments or investigations, linking cause and effect **e.g. We found out that the length of the wire does affect the brightness of the bulb.**	• Identify patterns in data presented in various formats, including line graphs **e.g. The line graph from the data logger shows that as the wire length goes up, the light level goes down.** • Identify scientific evidence they have used in drawing conclusions **e.g. The length of wire does affect the bulb brightness because the graph shows the longer the wire, the dimmer the bulb.**	• Provide straightforward explanations for differences in repeated observations or measurements **e.g. Even if the crocodile clips were only a little bit out of position on the wire length, that could have affected the results.** • Draw valid conclusions that utilise more than one piece of supporting evidence, including numerical data and line graphs **e.g. We know that the length of wire affects the brightness of bulb because we saw it, we measured it and the graph shows it too.**

Task 8 Burger Chain

APP	National Curriculum Programme of Study: Sc2 5d,e
AF1	QCA Scheme of Work: 6a
AF3	

Task overview

Research-based investigation using secondary sources to identify elements of interdependency in a food web.

Key concepts

• Interdependence
• Food chains and webs

Outcomes

• Children prepare flow chart showing elements of a food web resulting in a burger meal.
• They also prepare a food chain/web for living things in a school grounds.

Resources

• access to library resources and/or Internet
• photos of typical burger chain meal or cartons from a burger chain
• Task 8 Pupil Sheets

Teaching notes

• Set the scene for the task by discussing visits children might have had to burger restaurants and the contents of a typical burger meal. Show photograph of burger meal and ask children to list what the food stuffs are.

• Discuss the statement made by Dan on the Pupil Sheet. *Is he right?*

• From each individual food ingredient, challenge them to track back the food chain to the source using library resources or the Internet. Model an example for them such as:

grass ⟶ cow ⟶ Alfie
　　　　 (beef and milk)

• Can they identify all of the plants, all of the primary consumers, all of the secondary consumers?

• Are there any plant sources that surprised them, sugar for example?

• Children represent the food chains and webs as flow charts or diagrams and explain how green plants are needed to produce a burger meal.

• Explore the outside environment and ask children to make a list of all the living things they find. Can they identify the producers and consumers? Now ask them to choose one living thing and include it in a food chain, e.g.

leaves ⟶ earthworm ⟶ blackbird ⟶ domestic cat ⟶ decomposing bacteria

Task 8 Burger Chain

Alfie and Dan are in a burger restaurant enjoying a meal. 'Y'know,' said Alfie, removing shreds of lettuce from his burger, 'I could do without this foliage getting in the way of the meat, particularly the gherkins! I mean, when you think about it, we would all be better off without the green stuff.'

'Where I agree with you about the gherkin,' nodded Dan, 'I think you'll find that without the green stuff there would be no burger, no bun, no ketchup, no fries and no cola either!'

Is Dan right?

What you need to do

• Draw a food chain or web as a flow diagram or chart to explain to Alfie why green plants are necessary in order for him to get his meal.

• Explore your schools grounds and make a list of the living things you can find. Choose one and construct a food chain that includes it.

You may find these words helpful

food chain, food web, producer, consumer, interdependence, green plants, sun

Task 8 Burger Chain

	Level 3 — Across a range of contexts and practical situations pupils:	Level 4 — Across a range of contexts and practical situations pupils:	Level 5 — Across a range of contexts and practical situations pupils:
AF1 Thinking scientifically	• Identify differences, similarities or changes related to simple scientific ideas, processes or phenomena **e.g. can distinguish between green plants and animals** • Represent things in the real world using simple physical models **e.g. understands that food chains represent feeding relationships**	• Use scientific ideas when describing simple processes or phenomena **e.g. can talk about producers and consumers in a food chain** • Identify scientific evidence that is being used to support or refute ideas or arguments **e.g. We used keys to identify living things in the school grounds and decide which group they belonged to.**	• Use abstract ideas or models or more than one step when describing processes or phenomena **e.g. understands that food chains link in webs and that removing one element affects all the others** • Identify the use of evidence and creative thinking by scientists in development of scientific ideas **e.g. We worked out that if there were no green plants in the school grounds then the animals would not be able to survive.**
AF3 Communicating and collaborating in science	• Present simple scientific data in more than one way, including tables and bar charts **e.g. draws simple flow chart** • Identify simple advantages of working together on experiments or investigations **e.g. Each group did their fieldwork in a different area so we could cover the whole school grounds.**	• Select appropriate ways of presenting scientific data **e.g. draws flow chart correctly labelled with producers and consumers identified** • Identify simple advantages of working together on experiments or investigations **e.g. By working together we are able to check each other's results.**	• Decide on most appropriate formats to present sets of scientific data, such as using line graphs for continuous variables **e.g. draws food web and identifies points of overlap and interdependence** • Suggest how collaborative approaches to specific experiments or investigations may improve the evidence collected **e.g. Scientists in different environments, such as rainforests and polar regions, are collecting evidence of how living things are linked in similar ways.**

Task 9 Dodgy Kebab

APP	National Curriculum Programme of Study: Sc1 2b,e Sc2 5f
AF2	QCA Scheme of Work: 6b
AF4	

Task overview

An investigation into food hygiene and use of disinfectants.

Key concepts

• Assessing risks
• Fair test
• Using evidence

Outcomes

• Children prepare a letter to takeaway owner with recommendations on how to prevent food poisoning in his takeaway.
• They include experimental evidence to back up their recommendations.

Resources

• slices of bread
• sealable bags
• plant sprayer with water
• disinfectant sprays/antibacterial sprays
• acetate marked with 1 cm square grid
• tongs
• Task 9 Pupil Sheets

Teaching notes

• Set the scene for the task by discussing the picture on the Pupil Sheet and what the Environmental Health Officer might have said in his report. What do children know about how diseases spread? Can they identify any food hygiene risks in the kebab shop? What would they advise the owner to do or to change and why?

• Tell children they need experimental evidence to back up their claims so they are going to investigate mould growth on bread. *What is mould? Is it safe to eat mouldy food?*

• Do children have any ideas on how they could organise this investigation? What do they need to do to keep safe when growing moulds?

• Children conduct own investigation or could be directed as follows:

   o Use slices of plain bread. For the first slice, remove with tongs, spray lightly with water and place in a sealable bag. For the second slice, thoroughly handle it (to transfer microbes from hands to the bread), spray lightly with water and place in a bag. With the third slice do the same as the second but spray with an anti-bacterial spray.

   o Pin bags to a display board for easy observation (making sure the body of the bag is not pierced). Periodically take down and count the spread of the mould growth using the acetate grid (see resources). Children can graph this for each sample.

• What do they notice about the rates and spread of mould on the bread samples? Are the anti-bacterial/disinfectant products successful at preventing decay?

• **Keep Safe! Dispose of contaminated bread safely by submerging sealed bags in disinfectant solution then opening the bags underwater to flood with solution. Leave overnight then throw away.**

• Children prepare letter to kebab shop owner with their recommendations and evidence.

Task 9 Dodgy Kebab

After the football match, Jamie bought a kebab from the local takeaway. It was delicious. However, the next day he felt really ill and the doctor said he had food poisoning.

The Environmental Health department sent an inspector to the takeaway to advise the owner about food hygiene. These are some of the things he noticed:

What you need to do

• Write a letter to the takeaway owner explaining what causes food poisoning and what he can do to make his takeaway more hygienic.

• Carry out an investigation over time to show the effects of mould growth on bread. Use your results to back up your advice to the takeaway owner.

You may find these words helpful

microbe, mould, bacteria, temperature, spread

Task 9 Dodgy Kebab

	Level 3 Across a range of contexts and practical situations pupils:	Level 4 Across a range of contexts and practical situations pupils:	Level 5 Across a range of contexts and practical situations pupils:
AF2 **Understanding the applications and implications of science**	• Explain the purposes of a variety of scientific or technological developments **e.g. We use disinfectants to get rid of germs.** • Identify aspects of our lives, or of the work that people do, which are based on scientific ideas **e.g. To be healthy we need to keep food preparation areas clean and keep food fresh.**	• Describe some simple positive and negative consequences of scientific and technological developments **e.g. Understanding disease causing microbes has helped us to be healthier but some people in extremes may become frightened of touching anything in case they catch a disease.** • Identify aspects of science used within particular jobs or roles **e.g. knows that Environmental Health Officers need to know about how microbes and diseases spread and how food decays**	• Describe different viewpoints a range of people may have about scientific or technological developments **e.g. can give a range of benefits of use of microbes (food production, medicine) and the costs (introduction of chemicals to food to delay decay etc)** • Link applications of science or technology to their underpinning scientific ideas **e.g. talks about how improvements in sanitation, refrigeration, hygiene and bacteriological control have improved food quality standards and 'shelf-life'**
AF4 **Using investigative approaches**	• Identify one or more control variables in investigations from those provided **e.g. We made sure we all tested the same brand of bread.** • Recognise obvious risks when prompted **e.g. I shouldn't touch the mouldy bread.**	• Decide when it is appropriate to carry out fair tests in investigations **e.g. We knew it was important to do all of our tests in the same way.** • Identify possible risks to themselves and others **e.g. I should wash my hands thoroughly to remove any mould from them before I touch anyone or anything else.**	• Recognise significant variables in investigations, selecting the most suitable to investigate **e.g. We wanted to test whether anti-bacterial sprays affected mould growth on bread so we tested each type.** • Make, and act on, suggestions to control obvious risks to themselves and others **e.g. The bread can still be dangerous after we've finished investigating so we should make sure we dispose of it safely.**

Task 10 A Powdery Problem

APP	National Curriculum Programme
AF2	**of Study:** Sc3 1a, 2a,d,f
AF4	**QCA Scheme of Work:** 6c

Task overview

An investigation to identify the difference between four white powders.

Key concepts

• Planning an investigation
• Identifying similarities and differences
• Dissolving

Outcomes

• Children write a crime lab report for Inspector Bleu explaining how they identified the sample and who the culprit is.

Resources

• a selection of white powders, which could include:
  ○ cornflour
  ○ bicarbonate of soda
  ○ white powder paint
  ○ crushed chalk
• water
• white vinegar or lemon juice
• test tubes or plastic cups
• spoons
• digital balance
• measuring cylinders
• digital camera
(Children may come up with some other items to mix with the samples, if possible allow them access to these too.)
• Task 10 Pupil Sheets

Teaching notes

• **Keep Safe! Warn children not to taste any of the samples.**

• Prior to lesson, set out the four samples taken from the suspects' houses (see Pupil Sheet) and label with the name of suspect. Choose a sample of one of the powders to be used as the crime-scene powder.

• Set the scene for the task by talking through what Inspector Bleu's dilemma is. Allow children 5 minutes of discussion time in their groups before bringing discussion to whole class. In what way could they identify differences between the samples of powder? Elicit prior knowledge on solids dissolving in liquids. *Could we use this knowledge to match the suspect powder to the samples? How else could we test the powders?*

• Discuss with children how they will observe the differences between the powders and what method of recording they could choose to make.

• *How will we make the test fair? If the powder is the variable we are changing which others must we keep the same?*

• Record results in a table and use photos from a digital camera to illustrate the results.

• Encourage children to investigate all of the samples before allowing them to compare them to the crime scene sample.

• Children prepare report for Inspector Bleu.

• *Oh no! The suspect sample was accidentally all used up – we need to retrieve some of it for evidence!* Ask children to think of ways we might get the suspect's powder back (filtering or evaporation depending on whether it has dissolved). This might be an investigation you can do at another time.

• Write up results in a lab report to Inspector Bleu.

• *NB:* Other white powders you could use include cream of tartar, icing sugar and potato flour.

Task 10 A Powdery Problem

Inspector Bleu of the French police is in a bit of a pickle, the Mona Lisa has been stolen! The only evidence of who took it is a small pile of white powder found under where the painting once hung.

He has four suspects: Monsieur Boulange, Madame Peintre, Mademoiselle Noir and Monsieur Saler. He has found samples of powder from each of their houses and would like them to be tested.

Inspector Bleu has heard that your class are fantastic science investigators and wonders if you could match the powders?

Can you help Inspector Bleu by investigating the powders for him?

What you need to do

• In groups discuss how you are going to carry out the investigation.
• Write a report to Inspector Bleu when you have completed the investigation, stating what you did and who he should arrest for the theft.

You may find these words helpful

solid, liquid, mix, dissolve, solution, solute, suspension, floated, undissolved, fizzed, particles, reaction, results, observations

Task 10 A Powdery Problem

	Level 3 Across a range of contexts and practical situations pupils:	Level 4 Across a range of contexts and practical situations pupils:	Level 5 Across a range of contexts and practical situations pupils:
AF2 **Understanding the applications and implications of science**	• Link applications to specific characteristics or properties **e.g. I will look to see what happens to the powder when I mix it with water.** • Identify aspects of our lives, or of the work that people do, which are based on scientific ideas **e.g. can recognise science used by the police to catch criminals**	• Recognise applications of specific scientific ideas **e.g. I can identify the powder by seeing how it reacts with water.** • Identify aspects of science used within particular jobs or roles **e.g. can recognise that science in used in forensics, although not necessarily the methods being used in the investigation**	• Link applications of science or technology to their underpinning scientific ideas **e.g. can recognise that some of the powders can be identified through their understanding of solids in solution or suspension** • Indicate how scientific or technological developments may affect different groups of people in different ways **e.g. can recognise how more sophisticated methods could aid forensics and be a more accurate identification**
AF4 **Using investigative approaches**	• Identify one or more control variables in investigations from those provided **e.g. We will add the same amount of each powder to the water.** • Select equipment or information sources from those provided to address a question or idea under investigation **e.g. is given the equipment to filter the different materials**	• Decide when it is appropriate to carry out fair tests in investigations **e.g. We will be keeping all other variables the same but changing the powder we add to the water and observing the effect.** • Select appropriate equipment or information sources to address specific questions or ideas under investigation **e.g. is able to say what equipment they will need from those provided**	• Recognise significant variables in investigations, selecting the most suitable to investigate **e.g. There are several different ways we could attempt to identify the different powders but we think that observing the reaction with water will be the most straightforward and useful for us to begin with.** • Explain why particular pieces of equipment or information sources are appropriate for the questions or ideas under investigation **e.g. is able to use a filter paper to separate materials as opposed to a sieve**

Task 11 Hotto Choco

APP	National Curriculum Programme of Study: Sc3 1a, 2b,c,d
AF3	QCA: 6d
AF4	

Task overview

Children investigate if the percentage of cocoa solids in chocolate affects how quickly it melts.

Key concepts

• Melting
• Reversible changes
• Collecting evidence
• Drawing conclusions

Outcomes

• PowerPoint report for Hotto Choco company including graphs of results.

Resources

• chocolate bars containing different percentages of cocoa butter (usually shown on the wrapper as a % figure)
• cake casings
• warm water in large bowl NOT boiling water.
• timers
• wooden lollipop sticks
• thermometers
• digital scales to measure mass of chocolate
• PowerPoint
• Task 11 Pupil Sheets

Teaching notes

• Chocolate usually melts at around body temperature 36°C or 37°C

• Discuss the problem faced by the Hotto Choco company. Give children squares of different chocolate to explore. Note the sound of the chocolate as it snaps. Darker chocolate with a higher percentage of cocoa solids will give a clear 'snap' as it breaks.

• Check for understanding of the term *per cent* as being equal parts per hundred. Explain that one ingredient which varies between the different bars is the percentage of cocoa solids.

• *If the percentage of cocoa solid is one variable in the investigation, what are the other variables that we must keep constant while we investigate?*

• Ask children how we could safely melt chocolate in the classroom while observing the changes. Remind children of how chocolate is melted when cooking. Explain that we will put the chocolate into the cake casings and float them on the warm water.

• Discuss with children what measurements they must take (time in seconds) and how to check that the chocolate is fully melted. (Each group to use a wooden lollipop stick to push into the chocolate to check it has fully melted.)

• Allow children time to discuss how they will make the investigation fair. Discuss how they will check that their results are accurate. Should they repeat the investigation?

• *How will you chart your results? Which is the most appropriate method?*

• Following the investigation check that children are aware that the more cocoa solid in the chocolate the longer it takes to melt.

Task 11 Hotto Choco

The chocolate company, Hotto Choco, was in panic over claims that its Rock Choc bar is melting in stores.

Can you find which chocolate melts the quickest?

What you need to do

• In groups investigate how quickly different chocolate samples melt.

• Create a PowerPoint presentation explaining what you did, showing your results and advising Hotto Choco on what sort of chocolate they need to use in their products.

You may find these words helpful

temperature, melt, melting, percentage, time, minutes, seconds

Task 11 Hotto Choco

	Level 3 Across a range of contexts and practical situations pupils:	Level 4 Across a range of contexts and practical situations pupils:	Level 5 Across a range of contexts and practical situations pupils:
AF3 **Communicating and collaborating in science**	• Present simple scientific data in more than one way, including tables and bar charts **e.g. can present data in a bar chart and then ranked list** • Identify simple advantages of working together on experiments or investigations **e.g. We were able to investigate all the chocolate types because working together meant we worked quicker.**	• Select appropriate ways of presenting scientific data **e.g. uses a bar chart or line graph to present data** • Use appropriate scientific forms of language to communicate scientific ideas, processes or phenomena **e.g. recognises that the process is melting and that it is caused by heating the chocolate**	• Decide on the most appropriate formats to present sets of scientific data, such as using line graphs for continuous variables **e.g. can use data to produce a line graph with % cocoa solid plotted against time and can use this to predict values for intervals not tested directly** • Suggest how collaborative approaches to specific experiments or investigations may improve the evidence collected **e.g. Almost every group agreed on the same pattern in the amount of cocoa solids in the chocolate and how long it took to melt so our evidence should be reliable.**
AF4 **Using investigative approaches**	• Make some accurate observations or whole number measurements relevant to questions or ideas under investigation **e.g. The milk chocolate had melted completely after 2 minutes and 58 seconds.** • Recognise obvious risks when prompted **e.g. The water is hot water.**	• Make sets of observations or measurements, identifying the ranges and intervals used **e.g. The chocolate containing 35% cocoa solid melted completely after 2 minutes and 58 seconds while the chocolate containing 80% cocoa solid took 4 minutes and 20 seconds to melt completely.** • Identify possible risks to themselves and others **e.g. The water may be hot so we need to be careful not to spill it.**	• Repeat sets of observations or measurements where appropriate, selecting suitable ranges and intervals **e.g. is aware of the need to repeat the investigation to ensure accurate data. Is able to use smaller units of time/parts of seconds** • Make, and act on, suggestions to control obvious risks to themselves and others **e.g. We will make sure chairs are tucked under table and will act sensibly around the hot water to ensure that no spilling of water happens.**

Task 12 Trapeze Trouble

APP	National Curriculum Programme of Study: Sc1 2e Sc4 2b,c
AF4	QCA: 6e
AF5	

Task overview

Investigation into how the course of swinging objects changes depending on mass. Consideration of how science can inform health and safety plans.

Key concepts

- Assessing risks
- Forces
- Fair test
- Using evidence
- Repeating measurements
- Reliability of results

Resources

- 1 metre length of string securely attached to a toy bucket
- objects of different weights (masses)
- stopwatches
- rulers
- Task 12 Pupil Sheets

Outcomes

- Health and safety report advising whether Monsieur Muscle should perform on the trapeze.

Teaching notes

- Set the scene for the task by discussing the dilemma faced by Mr Master (see Pupil Sheet) and make sure that everyone knows that the flying trapeze is a circus act where the performer performs tricks from a swinging bar suspended by ropes. Talk and find out about Jules Léotard who first invented the flying trapeze in 1859.

- Demonstrate how the trapeze can be modelled using a toy bucket suspended on a string. Discuss which forces are acting on the 'trapeze'.

- Predict whether different masses in the bucket will affect the swing of the bucket. How could they measure the swing (e.g. the time taken for 10 swings or how many swings in a given time)?

- Ask children to identify hazards and carry out a risk assessment. If necessary, help children to set up the fair test investigation to test a range of masses.

- **Keep safe! The bucket should be securely tied to string by an adult. Children should take care that the bucket does not collide with anyone or anything.**

- Discuss how results could be presented e.g. which type of graph would be appropriate? *How could the reliability of the results be improved?*

- Children prepare a health and safety report for Mr Master, the circus owner. Can they suggest improvements to their investigation or identify any other related investigations to research?

Task 12 Trapeze Trouble

Disaster! Tina Trapeze has broken her arm and cannot perform her high-flying act. Circus strongman, Monsieur Michel Muscle, wants to replace Tina.

Michel is a large man and weighs twice as much as Tina. The circus owner, Mr Master, thinks that the swinging pattern of the trapeze will change and this could be a serious health and safety issue.

Can you help Mr Master decide whether Michel should perform on the trapeze?

What you need to do

• Carry out a risk assessment. What do you need to do to keep safe?

• Carry out a fair test to investigate if the trapeze swing changes when different objects of different masses are swinging.

• Prepare a health and safety report for Mr Master, which includes your test results.

You may find these words helpful

forces, push, pull, gravity, air resistance, length, weight, mass, timing, table, graph, recommend

Task 12 Trapeze Trouble

	Level 3 Across a range of contexts and practical situations pupils:	Level 4 Across a range of contexts and practical situations pupils:	Level 5 Across a range of contexts and practical situations pupils:
AF4 **Using investigative approaches**	• Select equipment or information sources from those provided to address a question or idea under investigation **e.g. chooses sensible equipment from a selection which is appropriate to the task** • Recognise obvious risks when prompted **e.g. The bucket could hit someone when it is swinging.**	• Select appropriate equipment or information sources to address specific questions or ideas under investigation **e.g. is able to say that a stopwatch is better than a clock to measure time accurately** • Identify possible risks to themselves and others **e.g. If the bucket falls off the string or it hits anyone, someone could get hurt.**	• Explain why particular pieces of equipment or information sources are appropriate for the questions or ideas under investigation **e.g. can explain that a stopwatch is needed because it can measure the timing accurately to 0.1s** • Make, and act on, suggestions to control obvious risks, **e.g. I will make a barrier so that no-one can be hit when the bucket swings.**
AF5 **Working critically with evidence**	• Identify straightforward patterns in observations or in data presented in various formats, including tables, pie and bar charts **e.g. recognises that the larger mass swings slowly** • Suggest improvements to their working methods **e.g. I think we need to do our timing more carefully.**	• Identify patterns in data presented in various formats, including line graphs **e.g. recognises that the time taken for larger masses to swing is longer than that for smaller masses** • Suggest improvements to their working methods, giving reasons **e.g. We need to always do the swings in the same way, like starting to swing the trapeze from a definite, marked place.**	• Provide straightforward explanations for differences in repeated observations or measurements **e.g. recognises that the three repeat readings are unlikely to be exactly the same because of slight human errors when carrying out the test** • Evaluate the effectiveness of their working methods, making practical suggestions for improving them **e.g. Our timing and swinging weren't very accurate. The same person should swing the trapeze as starts the timer.**

Task 13 Bella's Back Yard

APP	National Curriculum Programme of Study: Sc1 1a,b Sc1 2e,f,g,h Sc4 3c
AF4	QCA: 6f
AF5	

Task overview

Investigation into which materials reflect most light.

Key concepts

- Reflection
- How light travels
- Data collection

Outcomes

- Children prepare note to Bella advising her on making her backyard lighter and brighter.

Resources

- selection of materials e.g. plastic mirror, aluminium foil (smooth and crumpled), white card, black card, corrugated card, house brick, cd case (clear plastic), ceramic plate (white), sweatshirt fabric, etc.
- torch or strong light source
- data logger with light level sensor
- tape measure or ruler
- Task 13 Pupil Sheets

Teaching notes

- Set the scene for the task by discussing why they think Bella's yard is so dark? *Why do you think Bella wants her backyard brighter?* Ask them whether they know of an outdoor place that never gets the Sun. *What is it like?*

- Can children suggest some ways that would make Bella's yard brighter? They may suggest painting the walls a brighter/lighter colour or adding features such as mirrored tiles. *Bella doesn't want to be surrounded on all sides with mirrors so what would be a compromise?*

- Children devise a fair test to see which materials or colours of materials reflect the most light.

- Use a data logger with a light sensor attachment to collect data.

- *How far from the sensor and light source should the material be placed?* The torch needs to shine past the sensor from behind on to the material so the sensor is picking up light reflected back from the test material.

- *How will your results be recorded – initially? What sort of graph would be best?*

- *How many readings should be taken and why?*

- What do children predict will be the most reflective material?

- Children write a note to Bella (possibly including a before and after sketch) to advise her on how to make the most of the light coming in to her yard.

Task 13 Bella's Back Yard

Bella has just moved in to her first flat and she's very excited. There's just one problem. The yard is really dark and dingy. She'd really like to brighten it up.

She'd thought about putting some electric lights outside but her dad said that it would be too expensive.

She knows that some materials absorb light and others reflect it.

Can you help Bella make her back yard lighter?

What you need to do

• Use the light sensor on your data logger to measure how much light different materials reflect. How can you keep your test fair?

• Predict what will be the most reflective materials? Are you right?

• Write a note to Bella telling her what she should do to make her back yard lighter.

You may find these words helpful

light, reflect, absorb, ray, material, scatter, light, shiny, dark, rough, smooth, colour

Task 13 Bella's Back Yard

	Level 3	Level 4	Level 5
	Across a range of contexts and practical situations pupils:	Across a range of contexts and practical situations pupils:	Across a range of contexts and practical situations pupils:
AF4 **Using Investigative Approaches**	• Identify one or more control variables in investigations from those provided **e.g. We need to put the torch in the same place each time.** • Make some accurate observations or whole number measurements relevant to questions or ideas under investigation **e.g. can measure the reflected light from a material using a data logger**	• Decide when it is appropriate to carry out fair tests in investigations **e.g. knows that a fair test will give the most accurate comparison of materials** • Make sets of observations or measurements, identifying the ranges and intervals used **e.g. can measure reflected light from a range of materials and round the readings up or down**	• Recognise significant variables in investigations, selecting the most suitable to investigate **e.g. can recognise that the majority of the most reflective materials were light coloured and suggests colour as a variable to investigate** • Repeat sets of observations or measurements where appropriate, selecting suitable ranges and intervals **e.g. can use three repeat readings for each material and calculate the average, rounding up or down appropriately**
AF5 **Working Critically with Evidence**	• Identify straightforward patterns in observations or in data presented in various formats, including tables, pie and bar charts **e.g. The paler materials reflected most light.** • Suggest improvements to their working methods **e.g. recognises that some measurements may not be accurate or that conditions e.g. someone casting a shadow, may influence the reliability of the test**	• Identify patterns in data presented in various formats, including line graphs **e.g. The higher the level of reflected light, the higher the bar on the graph.** • Suggest improvements to their working methods, giving reasons **e.g. suggests making more than one test and repeating measurements to be sure of the results**	• Interpret data in a variety of formats, recognising obvious inconsistencies **e.g. The bar chart shows that the paler materials reflected most light and the darker materials reflected least light, except for the shiny black card.** • Evaluate the effectiveness of their working methods, making practical suggestions for improving them **e.g. recognises the drawbacks of their testing methods and makes realistic attempts to control these such as re testing results that do not seem to fit with the pattern**

Task 14 Dodgem Newton

APP	National Curriculum Programme of Study: Sc1 1a,b Sc1 2a–m
AF1 AF2 AF3	Sc4 2d,e
AF4 AF5	QCA: N/A

Task overview

A complete investigation into how the mass of a vehicle affects how far it travels when something collides with it.

Key concepts

- Identifying variables
- Observing and measuring
- Collecting evidence
- Comparing and presenting results and drawing a conclusion

Outcomes

- Children write a report describing their investigation, what evidence was collected and drawing a conclusion.
- They include a line graph.

Resources

- toy vehicles e.g. lorries which can carry a load
- various masses (under 500 g for safety)
- measuring tapes or metre rules
- ramps
- sticky tape
- Newton's cradle (optional)
- Task 14 Pupil Sheets

Teaching notes

- Set the scene for the task by asking whether anyone has been on dodgem cars. Discuss what happens and how forces are involved. Children may have heard the story of Newton and the apple (gravity). He also studied the forces of motion. Show a Newton's cradle: a toy that illustrates some of Newton's laws of motion. *Newton didn't invent the toy though, it's a relatively new (1960s) invention!*

- *Time Travellers Incorporated (T.T.I.) wants Sir Isaac Newton to enjoy his time on the dodgems but to limit the distance that he travels when bumped by another car. Would including another person in the car help? What difference would their mass make?*

- Discuss how this situation could be modelled. *How could the 'attacking' vehicle always arrive with the same force to collide with Newton's vehicle? Could the vehicle always be pushed with the same force? Could it be launched, e.g. from a ramp? How much mass should the 'attacking' vehicle have?*

- Ask children to carry out a risk assessment.

- **Keep safe! Think about how to make sure that the mass does not hit anyone.**

- *Plan how to carry out a fair test. Make a prediction about how the mass inside the vehicle would affect the distance travelled.* How could children check that their results are reliable?

- Children use results to draw a line graph, come to a conclusion and compare with prediction.

- Discuss what went well with their test and how they could improve it.

- Children write a report about their investigation for T.T.I.

Task 14 Dodgem Newton

Time Travellers Inc. (T.T.I.) is bringing the famous scientist, Sir Isaac Newton, back from the 17th century to visit us in the 21st century. They want him to have fun after his journey through time!

He will visit a fairground and see how we use some of his ideas about forces. T.T.I. would like Newton to try out the dodgem cars, but are worried that because he is so small and light, his car will always crash into the side of the track when other cars collide with him.

T.T.I. would like you to find out whether the weight (mass) of another person in Newton's car could stop this happening.

What you need to do

• Investigate whether changing the mass carried in a dodgem car changes the distance it travels when it is bumped into.

• Write a laboratory report to T.T.I. explaining your investigation and what you found out. Include diagrams and a graph.

You may find these words helpful

forces, mass, weight, distance, variables, fair test, measure, table, line graph, conclusion

Task 14 Dodgem Newton

	Level 3 Across a range of contexts and practical situations pupils:	Level 4 Across a range of contexts and practical situations pupils:	Level 5 Across a range of contexts and practical situations pupils:
AF1 Thinking scientifically	• Respond to ideas given to them to answer questions or suggest solutions to problems **e.g. can link the imaginary scenario with carrying out a practical investigation** • Use straightforward scientific evidence to answer questions, or to support their findings **e.g. I used my results to decide whether my prediction was right.**	• Use scientific ideas when describing simple processes or phenomena **e.g. can identify at least one of the forces involved** • Identify scientific evidence that is being used to support or refute ideas or arguments **e.g. The car with most mass doesn't travel as far, so Newton wouldn't crash into the side of the track as often.**	• Use abstract ideas or models or more than one step when describing processes or phenomena **e.g. identifies the combination of different forces involved** • Recognise scientific questions that do not yet have definitive answers **e.g. The car with most mass doesn't travel as far, but it might depend on how fast the other car was going and on the friction of the floor.**
AF2 Understanding the applications and implications of science	• Link applications to specific characteristics or properties **e.g. recognises that dodgem cars must be made of strong material** • Identify aspects of our lives, or of the work that people do, which are based on scientific ideas **e.g. We can enjoy dodgem cars because they have been designed to use forces for fun.**	• Recognise applications of specific scientific ideas **e.g. understands that dodgem cars are designed using materials which will withstand the force of collision** • Identify aspects of science used within particular jobs or roles **e.g. People who design dodgem cars make sure that the speed and mass (weight) of the cars produces forces within safe limits.**	• Identify ethical or moral issues linked to scientific or technological developments **e.g. discusses whether dodgem cars should be used as they are not essential and can be dangerous** • Link applications of science or technology to their underpinning scientific ideas **e.g. The most important forces at work are forward pushes which speed the car up and friction which shows the car down.**
AF3 Communicating and collaborating in science	• Present simple scientific data in more than one way, including tables and bar charts **e.g. uses diagrams, a table and a bar chart to present results** • Use scientific forms of language when communicating simple scientific ideas, processes or phenomena **e.g. We predict the lightest car will travel furthest.**	• Select appropriate ways of presenting scientific data **e.g. uses diagrams, a table and a line graph to present results** • Use scientific and mathematical conventions when communicating information or ideas **e.g. can represent a force as an arrow**	• Decide on the most appropriate formats to present sets of scientific data, such as using line graphs for continuous variables **e.g. designs own table, can explain why a line graph is appropriate for this data** • Use appropriate scientific and mathematical conventions and terminology to communicate abstract ideas **e.g. can draw a diagram using arrows to illustrate the forces involved**

Task 14 Dodgem Newton

	Level 3 Across a range of contexts and practical situations pupils:	Level 4 Across a range of contexts and practical situations pupils:	Level 5 Across a range of contexts and practical situations pupils:
AF4 **Using investigative approaches**	• Identify one or more control variables in investigations from those provided **e.g. can identify that the same car should be used each time** • Recognise obvious risks when prompted **e.g. If I drop the weight (mass) it might fall on my toe and hurt me.**	• Decide when it is appropriate to carry out fair tests in investigations **e.g. understands that the effect of weight (mass) on distance travelled can only be fairly investigated if all other variables are kept the same** • Identify possible risks to themselves and others **e.g. If the weight (mass) falls out, it might hit one of us.**	• Recognise significant variables in investigations, selecting the most suitable to investigate **e.g. can control the method of launch, floor surface and car; change only the mass (weight) and measure the distance travelled** • Make, and act on, suggestions to control obvious risks to themselves and others **e.g. I will tape the weight (mass) in so it won't fall out and hurt us.**
AF5 **Working critically with evidence**	• Identify straightforward patterns in observations or in data presented in various formats, including tables, pie and bar charts **e.g. My bar chart shows that the heaviest weight (mass) in the car went the shortest distance.** • Describe what they have found out in experiments or investigations, linking cause and effect **e.g. can identify that the heaviest car went the shortest distance**	• Identify patterns in data presented in various formats, including line graphs **e.g. can identify that the graph shows how the weight (mass) of the car affects how far it travels.** • Identify scientific evidence they have used in drawing conclusions **e.g. The mass does affect how far the car travels because my results show that the lightest car went furthest.**	• Interpret data in a variety of formats, recognising obvious inconsistencies **e.g. One of the points on my graph looks like it is in the wrong place because it doesn't follow the general pattern.** • Draw valid conclusions that utilise more than one piece of supporting evidence, including numerical data and line graphs **e.g. My table and graph shows that the heavier the weight (mass), the shorter the distance travelled.**

Pearson Education Limited, a company incorporated in England and Wales, having its registered office at Edinburgh Gate, Harlow, Essex, CM20 2JE. Registered company number: 872828

www.pearsonschools.co.uk

Pearson is a registered trademark of Pearson plc

Text © Pearson Education Limited 2010

First published 2010

14 13 12

10 9 8 7 6 5

British Library Cataloguing in Publication Data

A catalogue record for this book is available from the British Library.

ISBN 978 0 435 03361 3

Typeset by Mike Brain Graphic Design Limited

Original illustrations © Pearson Education Limited

Illustrated by Andy Cooke

Cover illustration © Clive Goodyer

Printed in the UK by Ashford Colour Press

Acknowledgements

Every effort has been made to contact copyright holders of material reproduced in this book. Any omissions will be rectified in subsequent printings if notice is given to the publishers.

Licence for the use of the APP Primary Assessment Guidelines has been obtained from the Controller of HMSO and the Queen's Printer in Scotland.

Websites

There are links to relevant websites in this book. In order to ensure that the links are up to date, that the links work, and that the sites are not inadvertently linked to sites that could be considered offensive, the links can be accessed at www.pearsonhotlinks.co.uk. Search for APP for Science or ISBN 978 0 435 03361 3.